Special Learners in School

Offering a wealth of photocopiable resources for use with individual children or small groups, *Special Learners in School* provides a step-by-step programme to help practitioners support children with a range of special educational needs, and develop the skills which are fundamental to their learning in the mainstream classroom.

Competencies including active listening and observation skills, memory, comprehension of pattern and sequencing, positional and expressive language, body awareness and emotional intelligence are all key to ensuring a child's access to the school curriculum. Recognising that these can be particular areas of difficulty for pupils with SEND, this book provides a range of activities designed to engage and gradually develop children's use of auditory and visual memory, pragmatic and sensory skills. Easily accessible and differentiated for children at lower and upper levels of ability, practical examples and activities can be used immediately, or be adapted in line with students' abilities and progress.

This will be an invaluable source of inspiration and activites for learning support assistants, teaching assistants, teachers and SENCOs looking to support children in mainstream schools as they develop skills fundamental to their learning.

Catherine Routley has worked for over 20 years in the field of special needs, supporting individual children and developing training courses for Learning Support Assistants.

SPECIAL LEARNERS IN SCHOOL

Understanding Essential Concepts

CATHERINE ROUTLEY

LONDON AND NEW YORK

First published 2019
by Routledge
2 Park Square, Milton Park, Abingdon, Oxon OX14 4RN

and by Routledge
52 Vanderbilt Avenue, New York, NY 10017

Routledge is an imprint of the Taylor & Francis Group, an informa business

© 2019 Catherine Routley

The right of Catherine Routley to be identified as author of this work has been asserted by her in accordance with sections 77 and 78 of the Copyright, Designs and Patents Act 1988.

All rights reserved. The purchase of this copyright material confers the right on the purchasing institution to photocopy pages which bear the photocopy icon and copyright line at the bottom of the page. No other parts of this book may be reprinted or reproduced or utilised in any form or by any electronic, mechanical, or other means, now known or hereafter invented, including photocopying and recording, or in any information storage or retrieval system, without permission in writing from the publishers.

Trademark notice: Product or corporate names may be trademarks or registered trademarks, and are used only for identification and explanation without intent to infringe.

British Library Cataloguing-in-Publication Data
A catalogue record for this book is available from the British Library

Library of Congress Cataloging-in-Publication Data
A catalog record has been requested for this book

ISBN: 978-1-138-31249-4 (pbk)
ISBN: 978-0-429-45819-4 (ebk)

Typeset in Univers and Kohinoor by
Servis Filmsetting Ltd, Stockport, Cheshire
Printed and bound by CPI Group (UK) Ltd, Croydon, CR0 4YY

Contents

Introduction 1

Part 1: Level 1 activities

Section 1: Auditory memory

Auditory programme Level 1

Activity 1: Requesting objects by name 11
Activity 2: Requesting objects by attribute 12
Activity 3: Using prepositions *in on under* 13
Activity 4: Using prepositions *in on under* (cont'd) 14
Activity 5: Introducing *behind* and *in front of* 15
Activity 6: Introducing *beside* and *next to* 17
Activity 7: Introducing the preposition *between* 19
Activity 8: Double request commands 20

Section 2: Visual memory

Visual programme Level 1

Activity 1: Remembering objects 22
Activity 2: Finding the same 23
Activity 3: Recognising differences 25
Activity 4: Card sequences 27
Activity 5: Pictures and memory 28
Activity 6: Recall of object placement 30
Activity 7: Filling in the missing bits 32

Section 3: Pragmatics

Pragmatics programme Level 1

Activity 1: (a) Using visuals (b) Without visuals 34
Activity 2: What do you say? 36
Activity 3: Asking the right question 38
Activity 4: Replying to a question 40
Activity 5: Expressing preferences 41
Activity 6: Expressing feelings and expressing a reason 42

Section 4: Sensory perception
Sensory programme Level 1
Activity 1: (a) Touch box activities (b) Outside the touchbox 44

Part 2: Level 2 activities

Section 1: Auditory memory
Auditory programme Level 2
Activity 1: Repetition of sentences 47
Activity 2: Questions relating to simple text 49
Activity 3: Omitted words 50
Activity 4: Giving instructions 51
Activity 5: Following instructions 52
Activity 6: Answering questions 54

Section 2: Visual memory
Visual programme Level 2
Activity 1: Placing and finding objects 57
Activity 2: Noting visual details 59
Activity 3: Visual memory for words and letters 60
Activity 4: Recognising identical images 62
Activity 5: Reproducing images 63
Activity 6: Missing numbers and letters 64

Section 3: Pragmatics
Pragmatics programme Level 2
Activity 1: Logical ordering 66
Activity 2: Predicting events 68
Activity 3: Predicting reactions and feelings 70
Activity 4: Asking simple questions 71
Activity 5: (a) What's the right word? (b) What's the right question to ask? 72
Activity 6: Starting a conversation 74

Part 3: Additional ideas for working with pupils

Reading a new book 78
Differentiation and comprehension 80
Describing a picture 85
Learning to read with symbols 87
Inference skills 89
Learners with significant behaviour/language needs 93

Introduction

It would not be an exaggeration to state that the mainstream classroom today comprises of a wide range of special needs. Inclusive teaching is the buzzword, with the onus on teachers to differentiate the curriculum to meet the diverse needs of the class. Having engaged with many schools over several years, I have noticed the extent of their needs has deepened and pupils who, not so long ago, would have been educated in a special school or, at least have access to an in-house resource base, are now schooled almost exclusively within the mainstream. Responsibility for their day to day learning is increasingly the responsibility of LSAs who, due to budget constraints, do not receive sufficient specialist training. Access to the curriculum, when basic skills such as active listening, knowledge of positional language are far from secure, is not within their reach.

The book is a prescriptive one and some of the sections would appear to be repetitive. However, it is essential that pupils' learning is guided in a step-by-step manner (a) to consolidate previous learning (b) to have a secure base on which to base new learning and (c) to ensure graduated learning of new concepts. The programme would also be suitable for EAL pupils.

I am aware that many pupils designated as having special needs are pupils with ASD and, although this book is not specially targeted at this cohort, there are sections which could prove helpful such as pragmatics and focused listening.

The book is made up of four sections for Level 1 activities:

- Auditory memory
- Visual memory
- Pragmatics
- Sensory perception – for pupils who need to experience additional practical activities.

Level 2 has three sections.

The programme can be carried out with an individual or small group. It is recommended that regular daily sessions take place of approximately 20 minutes if the programme is delivered to an individual pupil. It is recommended to begin with using actual objects and to progress to object representation in the form of pictures. Depending on the children's progress, Level 1 and 2 activities need not be followed in strict order.

To encourage and extend concentration, listening and memory, the auditory section should always be carried out first. It would be advisable to wait until the pupil is secure in at least three of the activities in the auditory memory section in Level 1 before including the pragmatics programme. In the meantime, tasks in the sensory perception examples should be used.

When planning a programme, always start with a short recap of previous learning in which they had been successful as this helps the pupil to feel confident in tackling new learning. The session should ensure new learning takes place towards the middle of the session and always end with a task you know is within the pupil's capabilities.

Modelling of the requests referred to in the auditory section is essential, especially in the earlier stages. It should be noted that the programme is a guide; the practitioner may feel more examples are needed in each section to enable the pupils to achieve understanding.

Sections in further detail

Auditory memory

These activities are not only useful for increasing attention and memory but also for introducing vocabulary. Whenever possible, use vocabulary included in the current class national curriculum, e.g. Ancient Greece, Great Fire of London, animal habitats. There will be occasions when the child will pick out the object/picture that appeals most; should this become a problem, the item should be removed.

Instructions in this section range from simple requests to prepositions with double requests, with two different prepositions.

Visual memory

Although there is considerable emphasis on the auditory modality, visual and other sensory pathways should also be developed as they contribute to an overall understanding of expressive language. This section is devised to develop observation and visual impression of the world around them, which should add to their development of comprehension and expression of language. The sections include sorting and matching for colour, size, shape, picture matching, positional memory, recalling missing objects removed, sequencing.

Pragmatics

Social use of language is an essential skill to enable development of social skills, the use of language in appropriate circumstances, responding to others' feelings. This is an area of particular difficulty for pupils with special needs. It is also important academically, as many curriculum-based activities rely on working in groups and communication between peers.

Sensory perception

This is a small section which focuses on the development of touch and smell. This feature is not used as extensively as auditory and visual channels; however, it is useful in increasing general awareness. It helps to improve body awareness and to introduce vocabulary relating to touch and smell. It is recommended it is used with pupils who perhaps are not ready to respond to the Pragmatics section and who will benefit from sensory input. The examples are shown in Level 1.

Please note, the sessions shown are solely examples and planning will differ depending on the abilities and progress of the individuals or groups.

Below are two brief examples of sessions: (1) a pupil who is new to the programme at Level 1, (2) a pupil who is at a higher level or has experienced Level 1.

Level 1: example of (a) auditory memory, (b) visual memory, (c) pragmatics, (d) sensory perception

(a) Auditory memory

Place four familiar objects on the table e.g. ball, pencil, ruler, book, model of duck, piece of Lego®

Ask, 'Can you give me the ball?'

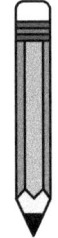   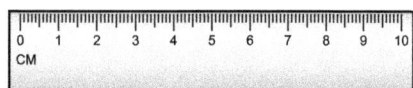

Increase objects to five familiar objects. Ask, 'Can you give me the duck?'

Increase to six. Ask, 'Can you give me the … book?'

Take two objects away, providing a choice of four. Ask, 'Can you give me the pencil and the ball?'

Increase to five objects. Ask, 'Can you give me the duck and the ruler?'

Increase to six objects. Ask, 'Can you give me the ball and the duck?'

Using four objects, request three objects. Ask, 'Can you give me the ball, the ruler and the duck?'

Increase to six objects. Ask 'Can you give me the ball, the duck and the ruler?'

(b) Visual memory

Put several different coloured objects of the same type on the table, e.g. cubes/counters. Give the child one object and ask, 'Can you find all the ones the same colour as this one?'

Put an assortment of objects on the table. Ask, 'Can you put all the ones of the same colour together?' Model how to sort them (it is advisable to use no more than four colours). For some pupils who need extra help, it may be helpful to have coloured boxes – red, yellow etc. – to reinforce the idea of the colour.

Put a selection of six shapes all the same colour on the table, e.g. three circles, three triangles, three stars. Hold up one of them and ask them to identify the shape. Ask, 'Can you find me one which is the same shape?'

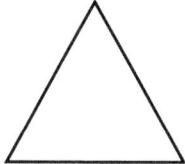  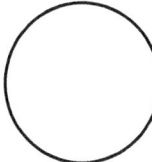

(c) Pragmatics

Ask, 'Your friend has fallen over in the playground. What do you think you would do?' (Choice of response provided by adult.)

Ask, 'You have found someone's jumper in the playground. What would you say to an adult?'

(d) Sensory perception

You will need a feely box/bag – either one which is commercially available or one can be made from a large box or bag.

Show pupils a variety of familiar objects (maximum four). Ask pupils to name them and place them in the box/bag. Ask, 'Can you find me the pencil?'

Show pupils a variety of familiar objects (a maximum of six). As referred to previously, ask pupils to name them and place them in the box/ bag . Ask, 'Can you find me the rubber?'

Show pupils a variety of objects (maximum eight) which have some similarities such as a flannel, washing-up cloth, plastic small animals (duck, bird,) two different Lego® pieces. Ask, 'Can you find me the smallest Lego piece?'

Level 2 examples (requests with two different prepositions)

(a) Auditory

Put four objects on the table. Ask, 'Can you put the … **on** the … and the … **under** the ….?'

Ask, 'Can you put the … **in** the … and the … in **front of** the ….?'

Increase to six objects – use of **beside/next** to and **between.**

Ask, 'Can you put the … **on** … the … and the … **beside** the ….?'

Ask, 'Can you put the … **in** the and … the … **behind** the ….?'

(b) Visual

Show pupils the table below for 10–15 seconds and then remove. Give pupils a blank table and ask them to draw in the objects.

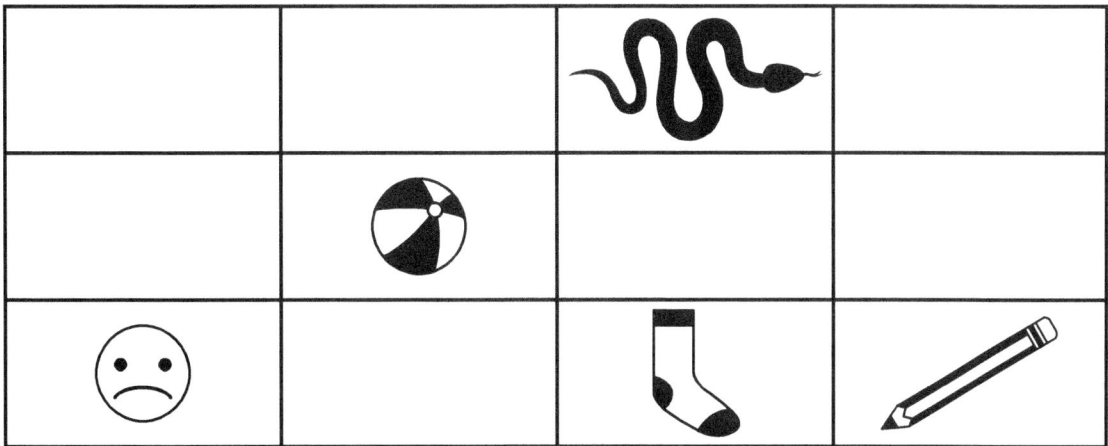

(c) Pragmatics

Show visuals individually. Pupil asks peer/adult (using visual as a prompt and checking the instruction has been correctly carried out):

(a) 'put the book on the chair' (b) 'put the book under the table' (c) 'put the pencils in the tin'
(d) 'put the book on the box' (e) 'put the ruler next to/beside the pencil' (f) 'put the sharpener in between the pencil and scissors'.

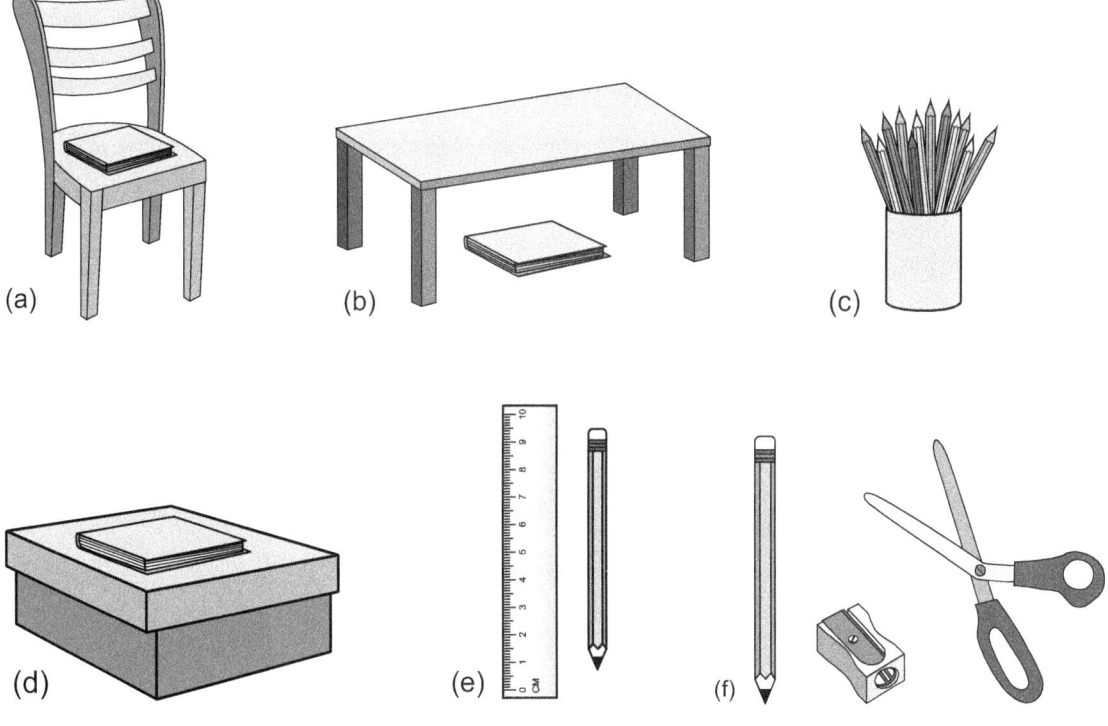

Part 1
Level 1 activities

Section 1:
Auditory memory

SECTION 1: AUDITORY MEMORY

Auditory programme Level 1

Activity 1
Requesting objects by name

(It is assumed the pupil has already successfully completed the exercise shown in the 'Level 1: example of (a) auditory memory' identified in the introduction section.)

(i) Requesting two objects by name

Provide pupil with three familiar objects e.g. 'brick, pencil, ruler' and request two of them. Ask, 'Can you first give me the pencil and then the brick?'

Using five objects, request two of them: 'Can you first give me the … and then the ….?' Using four objects, request three of them: 'Can you first give me the … then the … and then the ….?' Use concrete aids to scaffold memory e.g. fingers, counters. Ask the pupil to repeat the objects requested back to you to further scaffold memory.

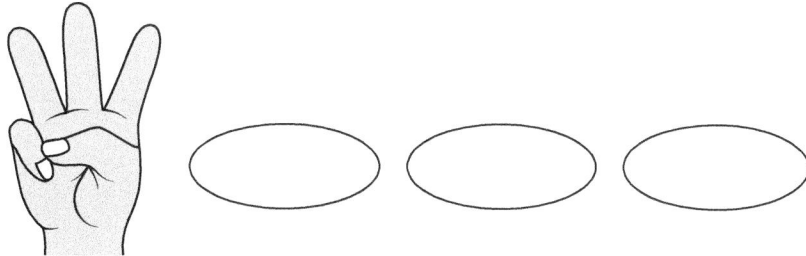

(ii) Requesting three objects by name

Using six objects, request three of them:

'Can you first give me the … then the …. and then the …'

(iii) Repetition of words (related): 'Can you please repeat the words after me?'

mouse cat   pencil pen   cake biscuit
lion tiger bear   jumper coat scarf   milk tea juice

Repetition of three-word sentences: 'Can you please repeat these sentences?'

I like shopping   I fell down   Beth can run   She likes swimming   Robert speaks loudly

PART 1: LEVEL 1 ACTIVITIES

Activity 2
Requesting objects by attribute

(i) Requesting object according to attribute e.g. colour

Using four objects of different colours e.g. red car, blue brick, green crayon, yellow circle, black counter, white chalk

　Ask, 'Can you give me something red?'
　Ask, 'Can you give me something yellow?'

Using two more objects of different colours e.g. black counter

　Ask, 'Can you give me something blue and something yellow?'
　Ask, 'Can you give me something black?'
　Ask, 'Can you give me something black and something green?'
　Ask, 'Can you give me something white and something blue?'

(ii) Ask pupil to repeat the following two words (unrelated)

　　box ship　　cake basket　　spoon window　　hamburger scissors　　paper curtain

And then three related words

　　lion tiger bear　　spoon knife fork　　orange lemon banana

Repetition of four-word sentences

　　I like shopping today　　John fell down backwards　　Beth can run fast
　　Kate likes mashed potatoes

Copyright material from Catherine Routley (2019), *Special Learners in School*, Routledge

SECTION 1: AUDITORY MEMORY

Activity 3
Using prepositions in on under

(i) Using three objects on the table e.g. box, book, piece of Lego®, pencil, ball, scissors.

Begin by modelling. Teacher sits on the table and asks, 'Where am I sitting?' 'I am sitting **on** the table.' Asks pupil, 'Where are you sitting?' Prompt if necessary '(I am) sitting **on** the chair.'

    Adult: 'I am putting the pencil **on** the book'

    Asks pupil, 'Can you put the book **on** the chair?' (indicates chair)

    Asks, 'Where is the book?' Response required 'on the chair'

    Asks pupil (indicates if necessary), 'What is **under** the table? (Adult has previously placed Lego® under the table)

Response prompting may well be required to help response, as initially pupil may respond 'Lego'. Required response is 'Lego (is) **under** the table.'

    Asks pupil, 'Can you put [e.g.] the book **under** the table?' Asks pupil, 'Where is the book?' Response required 'The book is **under** the table.'

    Shows pupil pencils/crayons in a box.

    Asks pupil, 'Where are the pencils?' Models response, 'The pencils (are) **in** the box'

(ii) Using four objects

    Asks pupil: 'Can you put the Lego bricks **in** the box?' 'Where is the Lego?' Desired response is correct use of preposition.

(iii) Place five familiar objects on the table e.g. book, scissors, pencil, Lego®, box. Asks pupil, 'Can you put the scissors **on** the book?'

    'Can you put the … **under** the ….?'

    'Can you put the …. **in** the ….?'

Always ask pupil where the object is to enable practice in using the preposition.

Copyright material from Catherine Routley (2019), *Special Learners in School*, Routledge

Activity 4
Using prepositions in on under (cont'd)

(i) Asking for placement of two objects

'Can you put the pencil and scissors **on** the book?'

'Can you put the book and Lego bricks **in the** box?'

'Can you put the pencil and book **in** the box?'

'Can you put the ….and the … **under** the … table?'

(ii) Description of placement by pupil

Adult places object **under** chair, asks pupil 'Where is the …?'

Adult places object **in** cupboard, asks pupil 'Where is the ….?'

Adult places object **on** table, asks pupil 'Where is the …?'

(iii) Ask pupil, 'Can you repeat these words?' (three unrelated words)

    ball horse drum   ship car glove   rain ring scarf

    apple bed shark   chair triangle finger   fly glass sock

Can you repeat these sentences? (three word sentences with negation)

    He isn't there   I don't swim   I can't see   She shouldn't say   John isn't cold

Copyright material from Catherine Routley (2019), *Special Learners in School*, Routledge

SECTION 1: AUDITORY MEMORY

Activity 5
Introducing behind **and** in front of

(i) Adult demonstrates by standing **in front of** a chair/door, **behind** a table: 'I am standing in front of the door' Asks pupil, 'Can you stand in front of the door? Where are you standing?' Response desired (prompt may be required) '(I am) standing **in front of** the door.'

Adult stands **behind** a chair: 'I am standing **behind** the chair.' Adult asks pupil: 'Can you stand **behind** the chair?' Where are you standing?' '(I am) standing **behind** the chair.'

Using four familiar objects

Adult asks:

'Can you put the book …. **behind** the ….?'
'Can you put the box … **in front of** the ….?'

Asking for placement of two objects

'Can you put the …. and the …. **behind** the ….?'
'Can you put the … and the … **in front of** the ….?'

(ii) Using six familiar objects

Adult places object **in front of** the …. Asks 'Where is the ……?'

Adult places object **behind** the …. Asks 'Where is the …?'

Asking for placement of two objects using **in front of** and **behind**

'Can you put the …. and the … **behind** the chair?'
'Can you put the …. and the … **in front of** the door?'

Placement with additional request

'Can you put the … and the … **under** the …. and give me the ….?'
'Can you put the …. and the …. **in front of** the … and give me the …?'
'Can you put the … and the … **behind** the … and give me the …?'

Copyright material from Catherine Routley (2019), *Special Learners in School*, Routledge

(iii) Repetition of four-word sentences

John is not crying   Patrick is the taller   I think mum knows

It is over there   Let's have some soup   I was lost yesterday

We were both hungry

Four related words (useful to give pupil a clue as to the category they belong to e.g. the first words are about drinks, the next is fruit etc.)

milk tea coffee juice   banana orange plum strawberry

potatoes carrots onions peas   shoe sock coat jumper

pen pencil ruler rubber   switch keyboard tablet screen

Four unrelated words

cinema sticky tape bottle boot   printer melon cake star

library map slipper pen   glove shop building dog

elephant ship cake cloud

SECTION 1: AUDITORY MEMORY

Activity 6
Introducing beside and next to

Sometimes **next to** is easier for the pupil to understand initially but when the concept is understood use **beside**. Both should be used interchangeably.

(i) Teacher stands **next to** a chair. Says to pupil: 'I am standing **next to** the chair. Can you stand **next to** the chair?' Pupil demonstrates, 'Where are you standing?' Response: '(I am) standing **next** to the chair.'

'Can you stand **beside** the cupboard? Where are you standing?' Response to include **next to/beside** the cupboard

Selection of four objects

'Can you put the … **next to** the ….?'
'Can you put the … **beside** the ….?'

(ii) Selection of six objects

Adult places pencil next to the book. Asks 'where is the pencil?' Pupil response, '**next to/beside the** …'

Adult repeats action, places brick next to cupboard. Asks 'where is the brick' Response as above.

Request placement of two objects

'Can you put the …. and the … **next to** the ……?'
'Can you put the … and the … **beside the** …?'
'Can you put the … and the … **behind** the …?'

(iii) Preposition with additional request for one object

'Can you put the pencil and ruler **next to** the book and give me the brick?'
'Can you put the … and … **beside** the book and give me the …?'
'Can you put the ruler and the … **under** the box and give me the …?'
'Can you put the …. and …. **next to** the ….and give me the …?'

Copyright material from Catherine Routley (2019), *Special Learners in School*, Routledge

(iii) Pupil is asked to repeat

    (a)   Five related words

        boy girl father mother uncle   sugar tea coffee chocolate soup

        potatoes carrots onions peas cabbage   cake biscuit cream chocolate sponge

        hand leg arm elbow neck

    (b)   Five unrelated words

        ladybird grass sky sand sheep   bird snake fork car eye

        canoe mouse nail paper box   file shop mountain beach

        cup carpet whale banana box leg

Copyright material from Catherine Routley (2019), *Special Learners in School*, Routledge

SECTION 1: AUDITORY MEMORY

Activity 7
Introducing the preposition between

Teacher demonstrates 'I am standing **between** the chair and table.'

(i) Ask pupil, 'Can you stand **between** the chair and the table? Asks pupil, 'Where are you standing?' (I am) standing **between** the chair and the table.' (prompt may be essential)

Use four objects

Ask pupil, 'Can you put the …. **between** the ….. and the ….'

Use six objects

'Can you put the …. **between** the …. and the …. and the …'

'Can you put the …. in **between** the … and the …. and the …?'

'Can you put the … **beside** the …?'

(ii) Adult places …. **between** the … and the …. and asks, 'Where is the …?' (response **between** the …. and the …)

Adult places …. **besides** the … and asks, 'Where is the …?'

Placement of two objects with additional request

'Can you put the ruler and the … **beside** the box and give me the ……?'

'Can you put the …… and … **between** the …. and … give me the …?'

'Can you put the …. and … in **front** of the … and give me the ….?'

'Can you put the … and …. **in front** of the …. and give me ….?'

'Can you put the …. and… **next to** the …. and give me the ….?'

Adult should ask pupil where the object is, if it is felt that is needed, to reinforce the pupil's understanding.

(iii) Repetition of five-word sentences

Please stop that noise now   I do not like swimming   Henry said he went yesterday
David left his blue scarf   I have not forgotten you   He laughed at the programme

Copyright material from Catherine Routley (2019), *Special Learners in School*, Routledge

PART 1: LEVEL 1 ACTIVITIES

Activity 8
Double request commands

(i) Double request commands with similar prepositions, placement in different locations.

Using six objects ensure pupil is secure with their naming.

'Can you put the pencil **under** the table and the ball **under** the chair?'

'Can you put the …. **on** the … and the …. **on** the …?'

'Can you put the …. **in** the … and the … **in** the …?'

'Can you put the … **in front of** the the … and the … **in front of** the …?'

'Can you put the … **behind** the … and the … **behind the** …?'

'Can you put the … **under** the … and the … **under** the ….?'

'Can you put the … **beside** the … and the … **beside** the …?'

'Can you put the …. **next to** the …. and the … **beside** the …?'

'Can you put the … **between** the …… and the … and …. and the … **between** … and the …?'

(ii) Repetition of six-word sentences

The three dolls were sold yesterday   I went swimming with two friends

The dog ate the tough meat   I was out late last night

The important football match was lost

Copyright material from Catherine Routley (2019), *Special Learners in School*, Routledge

Section 2: Visual memory

Visual programme Level 1

Activity 1
Remembering objects

(i) Adult places two familiar objects on the table. Asks pupil to look at them for five seconds. Covers them. Asks pupil, 'Can you remember them?'

Adult places three familiar objects on the table. Asks pupil to look at objects for five seconds. Covers them. Asks pupil, 'Can you remember them?'

Adult places four items on the table, asks pupil to look for five seconds. Covers them. Asks pupil, 'Can you remember them?'

Adult places six items on the table, asks pupil to look at them for five seconds. Covers them. Asks pupil, 'Can you remember them?'

(ii) Adult places three different objects on the table, asks pupil to look at them, covers them and takes two away. Asks pupil, 'Which ones have I taken away?'

Adult places two more different objects on the table, asks pupil to look at them, covers them and takes two away. Asks pupil, 'Which ones have I taken away?'

Adult places a further object on the table (six altogether), asks pupil to look at them, covers them and takes two away. Asks, 'Which ones have I taken away?'/ 'Which ones are missing?' (Always expand language wherever possible, in this case by using the word 'missing' when the pupil is able to complete the request without difficulty.)

If the pupil can do this without difficulty, try removing three items and ask if they can remember the ones taken away/missing?

Remember, it is essential to use familiar objects.

Copyright material from Catherine Routley (2019), *Special Learners in School*, Routledge

SECTION 2: VISUAL MEMORY

Activity 2
Finding the same

(i) Pupil and adult have two sets of four identical objects e.g. small car, circle, star, brick.

Adult holds up one object and asks, 'Can you give me one the same?' Always reinforce i.e. 'Yes, your car is the same as my one, it's a car.'

Adult holds up another object and asks, 'Can you give me one that is the same?, 'Yes, it's the same as this one. It's a brick, the same.'

Extends to six identical objects

Adult holds up pencil and asks, 'Can you give me one the same?'

(ii) Colour

Provide pupil with three shapes e.g. two red cars and one green car. Ask which one is different/not the same. Adult, 'Yes the green triangle is different it's not the same colour.'

Provide pupil with five cubes e.g. four green, one yellow. Ask, 'Can you tell me which one is different?' Extend response as above.

(iii) Shape

Ask pupil to find the one that is not the same/different e.g. three stars, one circle, all the same colour. Ask pupil, 'Can you show me which one is not the same?'

'Yes, the circle is not the same. It's different. The others are all the same, they are stars.'

Repeat exercise with e.g. four oblong shapes, one star, all the same colour. Ask pupil, 'Can you tell me which one is different?' Extend response as above.

Copyright material from Catherine Routley (2019), *Special Learners in School*, Routledge

(iv) Set out a row of four objects with one facing a different way e.g. cars, counters, bears.

Ask pupil to find the one that is different. If pupil finds this difficult, point out 'which one is looking/facing a different way?'

Row of five objects with one placed in a different direction Ask 'which one is different/not the same?'

Row of five pictures with one facing a different direction. Ask, 'Can you point to the one which is different? Can you tell me why it's not the same as the others?'

SECTION 2: VISUAL MEMORY

Activity 3
Recognising differences

(i) Show pictures one at a time. Ask pupil to look at picture and then ask how the pictures are different.

Pupil to point to the difference. Always supply vocabulary e.g. 'There are no flowers in these pictures/the flowers are missing.' 'Is the ball in the same place in the two pictures?'

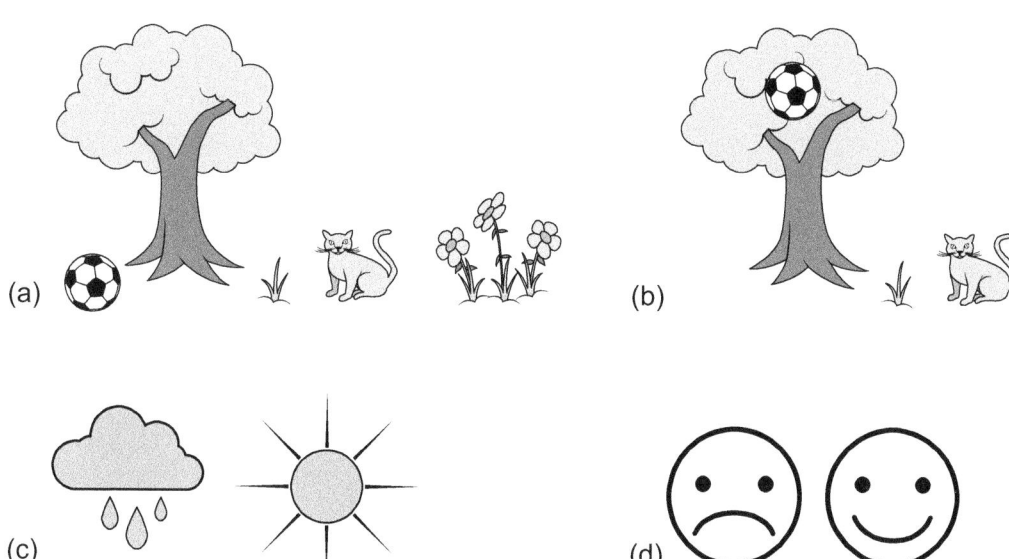

Again always supply the appropriate vocabulary and extend wherever possible, e.g., That's a disappointed (sad) face that's a delighted (happy) face, and ask for further description: 'Why do you think it's a disappointed face? Why is it a delighted face?' Or, e.g. 'Yes it's sunny in this picture. How do you think it makes everybody feel? What can they do now the rain has stopped?'

(ii) Using Lego®

(a) Show model below. Provide pupil with similar bricks and ask them to copy pattern with model on view. Ask, 'Can you copy my bricks?'

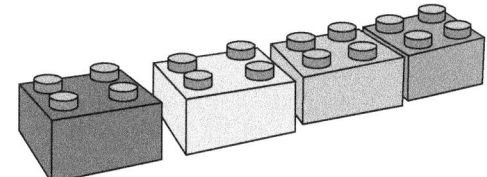

Copyright material from Catherine Routley (2019), *Special Learners in School*, Routledge

(b) Adult and pupil have identical bricks. Adult makes model and draws pupil's attention to the placing of bricks e.g. red brick is next to the blue brick. Hide model and ask pupil, 'Can you make one the same?'

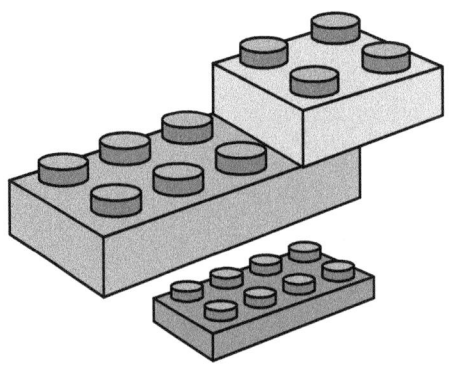

(c) Provide pupil with four bricks three different colours. Show model to pupil for about 10 seconds. Remove. Ask, 'Can you make one the same?'

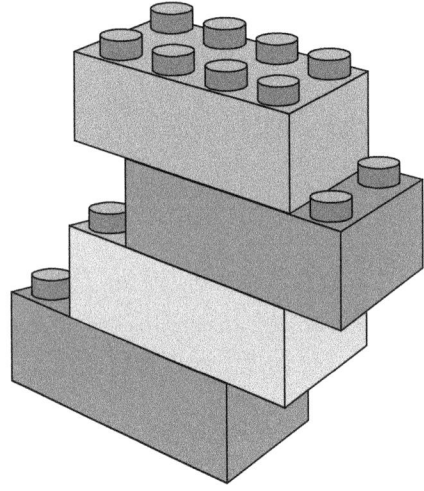

SECTION 2: VISUAL MEMORY

Activity 4
Card sequences

(i) Pupil and adult have three identical snap cards which are placed face up. Cards are named. Adult holds up card and asks, 'Can you show me one the same?'

Adult then asks, 'Can you show me one which is not the same/ different?'

Using same cards adult and child turn them over, face downward. Adult holds up one card from matching set and asks child 'Can you find one the same?'

(ii) Using four identical snap cards as above, name cards as they are turned over. Adult holds up one card from matching set and asks, 'Can you find one the same?'

Using five identical snap cards, ask question as above.

Using six cubes/bricks/cars/bears of different colours e.g. red/blue/red/blue, begin to make a sequence. Ask pupil to carry on with the sequence, making sure the colours are in the same order.

(iii) Following a sequence

    (a) using bricks (e.g. two bricks, one brick, two bricks), adult begins sequence and asks, 'Can you follow my sequence?'

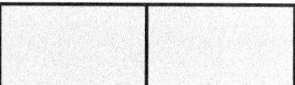  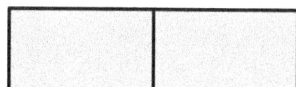

    (b) Sequence by shape

 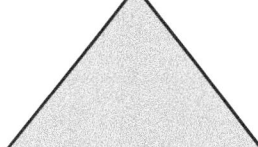 

Copyright material from Catherine Routley (2019), *Special Learners in School*, Routledge

PART 1: LEVEL 1 ACTIVITIES

Activity 5
Pictures and memory

(i) Show card to pupil for ten seconds. Pupil to name objects on card. Remove card and ask, 'Can you tell me the pictures on the card?'

(ii) Playing Pelmanism

Start with four duplicate cards. Pupil has to name cards and turn them over. 'Can you find two that are the same?' Always reinforce language: 'Yes they are the same', 'No they're different.' Increase to six or more duplicate cards. Pupil to find matching sets.

(iii) Show pupil two sets of pictures like the below, ask: 'Can you tell me how the two pictures are different?'

Copyright material from Catherine Routley (2019), *Special Learners in School*, Routledge

SECTION 2: VISUAL MEMORY

(iv) Show pupil a picture for approximately ten seconds. Draw attention to the number of apples in the tree, the position of the bird. Adult removes/covers picture and asks: 'Can you draw the same picture?'

Show pupil a picture for approximately ten seconds. Draw attention to the number of stars and their position. Adult removes/covers picture and asks: 'Can you draw the same picture?'

Copyright material from Catherine Routley (2019), *Special Learners in School*, Routledge

PART 1: LEVEL 1 ACTIVITIES

Activity 6
Recall of object placement

(i) Visual recall of placement of objects on table

Adult places three objects on table as in the figure below and draws pupil's attention to their position.

Cover/remove and ask: 'Can you remember where you should put them?'

Adult places three different objects on the table as in the figure below. Instructions as above.

(ii) Adult shows a picture. Pupil to look at it for ten seconds, adult covers it and asks: 'Can you draw the arrows?'

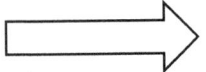 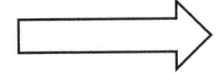 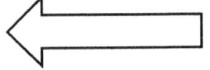 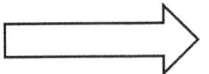

Use positional language to compare pupil's drawing with adult's e.g. one arrow is pointing a different way (direction).

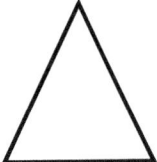  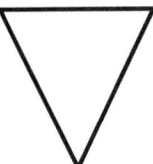 

Instructions as above. Use positional language e.g. the triangle is upside down.

Copyright material from Catherine Routley (2019), *Special Learners in School*, Routledge

SECTION 2: VISUAL MEMORY

Pupil is asked to look at a picture for ten seconds, after which the adult places the picture out of the pupil's sight. The pupil has to name the five objects.

Copyright material from Catherine Routley (2019), *Special Learners in School*, Routledge

PART 1: LEVEL 1 ACTIVITIES

Activity 7
Filling in the missing bits

Show pupil (a) for five seconds and then ask, 'Can you fill in the missing bits?' (from (b))

(a)

(b)

Pupil is shown each picture on the left individually. Adult removes it and asks 'Can you draw the same picture in the box?'

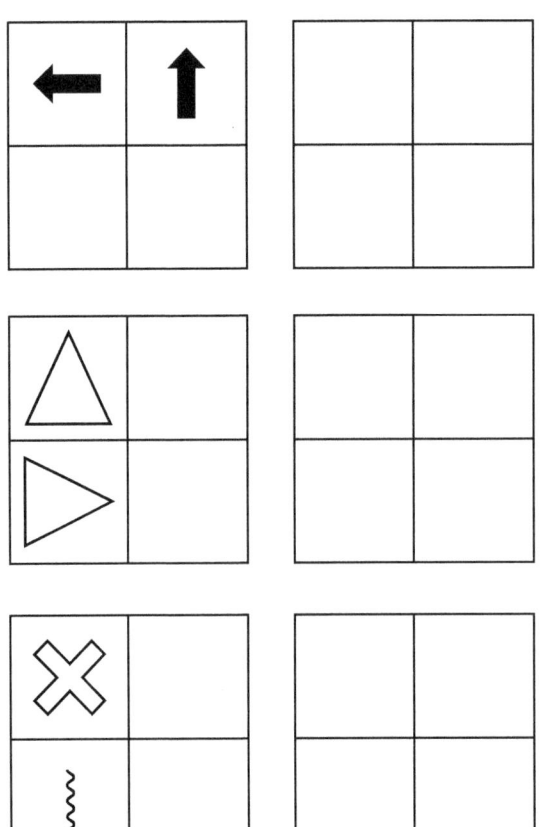

Copyright material from Catherine Routley (2019), *Special Learners in School*, Routledge

Section 3:
Pragmatics

Pragmatics programme Level 1

Activity 1
(a) Using visuals
(b) Without visuals

(a) Using visuals

(i) How do you feel? (provided with visuals above)

Ask pupil

> Show me the face which shows how you would feel when your teacher says 'You got all your spellings right'.
>
> (Prompt 'Yes, you would feel happy and you would feel pleased – that's another word for happy'.)

Repeat the feeling indicated, e.g. pleased: ask pupil, 'Can you tell me about a time when you have felt pleased about something?' If required, adult should supply pupil with a personal example.

> Show me the face which shows how you would feel when your teacher says she is cross with you because you haven't been listening during the lesson.
>
> (Prompt 'Yes, you would feel sad and you would feel sorry – that's another word for sad'.)

Repeat the feeling indicated, e.g. sorry: ask pupil to supply an example of when they felt sorry about something.

Copyright material from Catherine Routley (2019), *Special Learners in School*, Routledge

SECTION 3: PRAGMATICS

Show me the face which shows how you would feel when you hear your dog has gone missing. How do you feel?

(Prompt: 'Yes, you would feel sad/sorry and worried as well': ask pupil, 'Can you give me an example of when you have been worried about something?')

(b) Without visuals

(ii) How do you feel?

Ask pupil

You have broken a window with your football and someone shouts at you. How do you feel? (choice of two)

    nervous   thrilled

You wanted to a turn on the swing at the playground, but no one will let you. How do you feel?

    miserable   delighted

You wanted to be chosen for the class football team but you didn't get picked. How do you feel?

    disappointed   excited

You can't find your lunch box. How do you feel?

    upset   calm

Oh, you've just broken your friend's favourite new toy. How do you feel?

    hopeful   worried

Copyright material from Catherine Routley (2019), *Special Learners in School*, Routledge

Activity 2
What do you say?

(i) Ask pupil

Your teacher says she is cross with you because you keep forgetting your homework.

What do you say? (choice of two)

    Sorry it won't happen again.   I hate homework

You need to borrow a rubber. What do you say to your friend?

    Give me your rubber   Please can I borrow your rubber?

A bigger boy takes your ball and runs away so you can't play with your friend. What do you say?

    Can I have my ball back?   I'll hit you

You can't understand what someone is saying. What do you say?

    I am fed up with trying to listen to you   Can you please speak a little louder?

You really want to join in a game of football with your friends. What do you say?

    Please can I join your game?   You're all rubbish

Copyright material from Catherine Routley (2019), *Special Learners in School*, Routledge

SECTION 3: PRAGMATICS

(ii) Ask pupil: Is this a good thing to do?

    Pour water on a computer keyboard

    Open your door to strangers

    Wear your seatbelt when you are being driven

    Eat two bags of sweets all at once

    Throw rubbish in the playground

    Say thank you when someone gives you a present

    Cross the road when the light is red

    Go to bed late every night

    Be rude to a teacher

Copyright material from Catherine Routley (2019), *Special Learners in School*, Routledge

PART 1: LEVEL 1 ACTIVITIES

Activity 3
Asking the right question

(i) Questions: How do you ask?

Adult to pupil: Your mother says you can't have an ice cream as it's lunch time. What question do you ask?

   I don't care about lunch – can I have my ice cream?
   or
   Can I have an ice cream after lunch?

You are in in a burger bar and need some tomato ketchup.   What question do you ask?

   Please can I ……………………………………?

Anne can't find her watch. Her mother found it for her while she was at school. What question should she ask her mother?

   Where did ……………………………………?

You can't find your coat at home time.   What question do you ask your teacher?

   Where ………?

You find the noise of the music is too loud for you, how do you ask for it to be turned down?

   Can you ……….?

(ii) You can't find one of your gloves

   Ask pupil

   How would you ask for it? Would you say:

      'What is my glove?'   or   'Where is my glove?'

   Everyone has their topic book except you. What do you say?

      'Where is my topic book?'   or   'How is my topic book?'

Copyright material from Catherine Routley (2019), *Special Learners in School*, Routledge

Michael has hurt his finger and needs to find a bandage. What question should he ask his mother?

'Where can I find a plaster?'   or   'What can I find a plaster?'

PART 1: LEVEL 1 ACTIVITIES

Activity 4
Replying to a question

Ask pupil

'What do **you** say back (a reply)?'   (choice of two)

Your friend asks you 'What is your favourite sport?'

Do you say

'I like football /tennis best'   or   'I hate all sport'

Your classmate says 'I got good marks for my test'

Do you say

'Well done'   or   'So what?'

Your friend says 'Sorry I bumped into you'

Do you say

'You're clumsy'   or   'That's ok'

Your classmate says 'My birthday is tomorrow, I'm so excited'

Do you say

'Have a great day'   or   'What do I care?'

Sometimes you can win at games but not always. Your friend just beat you and you may feel like one of these

But what should you do?

Be a good winner or loser and say 'that was a .... game'

Copyright material from Catherine Routley (2019), *Special Learners in School*, Routledge

Activity 5
Expressing preferences

Objects

Ask pupil

'Can you tell me what you would sooner have and why?'

   A dog or a cat

   A bar of chocolate or a packet of crisps

   Watch *Star Wars* or go to the park

   A tablet computer or a television

   An ice cube or an ice cream

   A sleeping bag or a bed

   A cheese sandwich or a worm sandwich

   A box of chocolates or one chocolate

   A football or a rugby ball

   A bicycle or skates

Behaviour

Ask pupil

'Your friend won't share his computer with you during IT. What should you do?'

   Let the teacher know he is not sharing or try to push him out of the way

'A girl in another class is making your friend cry by calling her names. What should you do?'

   Tell an adult or hit the girl who is making your friend cry

'You have found some money in the playground. What should you do?'

   Put it in your pocket or give it to an adult

Copyright material from Catherine Routley (2019), *Special Learners in School*, Routledge

Activity 6
Expressing feelings and expressing a reason

Expressing feelings

Read sentence to pupil, ask them to complete it with how they would feel.

I had to go to the school welfare office today. I felt …….

I left my PE kit at home when it was time for PE. I felt ……

In English my teacher helped me to write a story. I felt ….

I had to run fast for the bus to get to school. I felt …..

I tripped over a school bag in class and everyone was watching. I felt …..

Mum said we are going to Disneyland for our holiday. I felt ….

The boy behind me keeps poking me in the back. I feel ….

I couldn't get any sleep last night, at school. I feel ….

The others in the class are so loud in this lesson. I feel …

My friends are making fun of me. I feel …..

I start my new school on Monday. I feel ….

Expressing a reason

Ask pupil 'Can you tell me if these sentences are silly or sensible and why?'

When you have made a cake, you put it in the oven to cook

I brush my hair with a spoon

I eat my breakfast in the morning

I clean my teeth with a fork

The cat eats corn flakes

My dog enjoys running in the park

I like to put my hot chocolate in the fridge

I like to go to the beach when it's hot

When it's cold I like to wear my shorts and sandals

I use my new pencil to write in my maths workbook

Copyright material from Catherine Routley (2019), *Special Learners in School*, Routledge

Section 4:
Sensory perception

Sensory programme Level 1

Activity 1
(a) Touch box activities
(b) Outside the touchbox

(a) Touch box activities

(i) Show children big and small circles and squares. Hide them in the touch box. Put a duplicate set on the table. Give pupil one and ask, 'Can you find another shape like this in the box?'

Show big and small triangles and rectangles. Hide them in the touch box. Put a duplicate set on the table. Give pupil one of these and ask, 'Can you find another shape like this in the box?'

(ii) Place a selection of objects in the touch box e.g. one wet, one rough, one cold, one sticky, one soft, one prickly.

Ask, 'Can you find one that feels e.g. soft /rough/cold?'

(iii) Give pupil materials with obvious textures e.g. felt, velvet, cotton. Put identical materials and two dissimilar ones in the touch box . Show them e.g. the felt materials and ask, 'Can you find another one like this?'

(iv) Have a selection of rough and smooth objects for child to feel e.g. glass bottle, soap, scourer, sandpaper, corrugated cardboard, leaf and ask, 'Can you find something which feels rough?'

Ask 'Can you find something that feels smooth?'

(b) Outside the touch box

(v) Have four identical pots or jars. Make three heavy and one light. Ask pupil to find the one that is different.

(vi) Have three pairs of identical pots and fill them with e.g. mints, coffee, shower gel. Hand one pot to pupil and ask, 'Can you find another one which smells the same?'

Copyright material from Catherine Routley (2019), *Special Learners in School*, Routledge

Part 2
Level 2 activities

Section 1:
Auditory memory

SECTION 1: AUDITORY MEMORY

Auditory programme Level 2

Activity 1
Repetition of sentences

Adult: 'I will be saying some sentences. Can you repeat them?'

(i) Five-word sentences

   Knights had swords and armour   Butterflies are found in gardens
   Some dogs live in kennels   I like to go shopping

   Six-word sentences

   Frogs and tadpoles live in ponds   In July the weather is warmer
   Playing out of doors is fun.   We went to the theatre yesterday

(ii) Repetition of **negative sentences**

   Four-word sentences

   It's not stuck fast   Don't come in yet   It's not torn badly

   Five-word sentences

   I didn't remember it properly   He's not coming until tomorrow   I don't think it's right
   I don't like strawberry jam   Reptiles don't have soft bodies

   Six-word sentences

   Polar bears don't like the heat   I was not lost last night   It didn't rain here until Sunday
   James' leg wasn't hurting until yesterday   He didn't think it's good enough

   Seven-word sentences (negative with solution)

   I can't stand the shouting, speak quietly   I can't see the boat, move nearer
   John doesn't feel well, take him outside

Copyright material from Catherine Routley (2019), *Special Learners in School*, Routledge

(iii) Positive and negative

John enjoyed the cartoon but didn't laugh much

We both like milkshakes but not strawberry flavour

She doesn't like to swim far, but enjoys diving

The lake isn't frozen yet, wait until January

Martin doesn't like vanilla ice cream, he prefers chocolate

Jade likes swimming, but doesn't enjoy running

Mel won't go to the cinema, but will go to MacDonald's

Andrew wants to go to the park, but won't play football

Activity 2
Questions relating to simple text

This is the first stage of comprehension, a literal understanding of the text using the words provided in the question, starting with one question.

(i) James went to the zoo on Wednesday.   *Where did James go?*

   The lion roared.   *Who roared?*

   Robert looked sad.   *Who looked sad?*

   I gave Sam a football.   *What did I give Sam?*

   I enjoyed learning about the Romans.   *Who did I enjoy learning about?*

   Mother made a delicious cake.   *What food did mother make?   How did it taste?*

   It was Jason's birthday and he was delighted to be going with his mother to the toy shop.

   Where did Jason go with his mother?   Why did he go with his mother?

(ii) Tom felt very hungry, so he made himself a large cheese and tomato sandwich.
   Why did he make some food?   What food did he make?

   Pat went to the supermarket to get some shopping for her mother.
   Where did Pat go? Why did she go?

   Tom wanted a strawberry milk to shake but they only had vanilla.
   What milkshake did Tom want? Did he get it?

   James went to the swimming pool, but it was closed. He felt very disappointed and had to go home.
   Why did James have to go home? Is this true?   James was happy the pool was closed.

Copyright material from Catherine Routley (2019), *Special Learners in School*, Routledge

Activity 3
Omitted words

(i) Ask pupil 'I am going to read you some words twice. On the second reading I will leave a word out.

Can you tell me which one it is?'

eggs bacon tomatoes	eggs bacon
shoes socks boots	shoes socks
pear apple banana	pear apple
tree bush flower	bush flower
book table window	book table
park pool tree	pool tree
hat coat jumper	hat jumper
eye aeroplane owl	eye owl
finger museum horse	museum horse
ball crayon chicken	crayon chicken

(ii) **Four words with one omitted**

fur canoe boat ship	fur canoe ship
hat duck bird spoon	hat duck spoon
brother tree bush desk	brother free desk
box arm corn chips	box chips arm
fog sand toe towel	toe towel sand

Copyright material from Catherine Routley (2019), *Special Learners in School*, Routledge

Activity 4
Giving instructions

(i) Ask pupil 'Can you stand up, get a piece of paper and pencil, write your name at the top and draw a happy face in the middle of the page? Draw a hat on the happy face.'

'Can you go and get me the book on the chair and open at page 5?'

'I am going to read to you some words which sound the same. Can you say either "same" or "not the same" to the words?'

bat hat	dog dug
house horse	bake bake
safe save	sand stand
give give	bed bet
book look	watch wash
crown clown	tip top
pat put	rot rat
sip sit	hen hen
mass miss	match mash

(ii) 'I will now read three words; can you tell me if they all sound the same?'

tall till tall	peg pig pig
walking walking waking	sink shrink shrink
skate stake skate	fist fast fist
ring rang rang	dances dance dances
flash flesh flash	when win when

Copyright material from Catherine Routley (2019), *Special Learners in School*, Routledge

PART 2: LEVEL 2 ACTIVITIES

Activity 5
Following instructions

(i) Ask pupil

'Can you draw a star in the middle of the T shirt and under it a small circle?'

'Can you colour one sleeve blue and the other one red?'

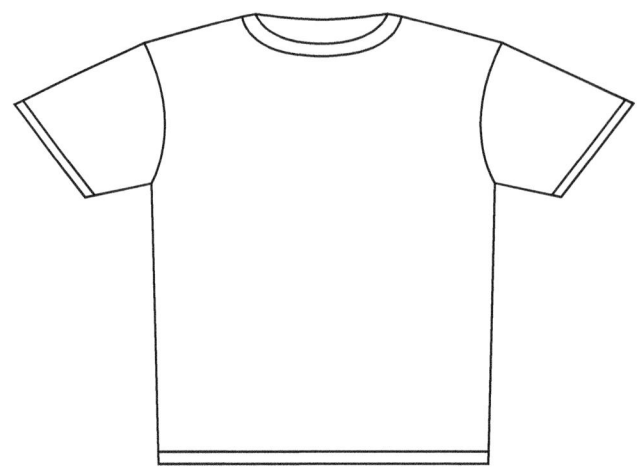

'Can you draw eyes on the boy and a mouth on the girl?'

'Can you draw a nose on the boy and eyes on the girl?'

'Can you draw a mouth on the boy, and a nose on the girl?'

'Can you draw glasses on the boy, earrings on the girl and colour her hair brown?'

'Can you give me your maths and topic book and get me the book on the chair by the window?'

'Can you put the red pencil, blue pencil and the ruler on the chair next to me?'

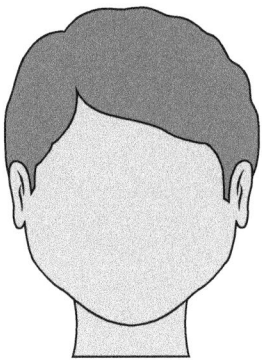 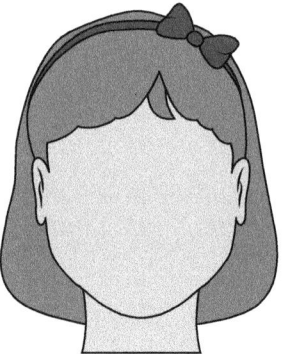

Copyright material from Catherine Routley (2019), *Special Learners in School*, Routledge

SECTION 1: AUDITORY MEMORY

(ii) Auditory association

Adult: 'I will say some words you know. Can you quickly say the first thing or things you think of when you hear each word?'

holiday	cake
sun	party
kitchen	lunch box
snow	lion
aeroplane	apple
car	biscuit
pizza	cat
school	fish
dog	chips
bird	television
shop	football

Activity 6
Answering questions

(i) Adult: 'I'm going to ask some questions. Can you think of a sensible answer?'

    What could you find growing in a garden?
    What could you find in a playground?
    What could you find in the sky at night?
    What could you find in a car?
    What could you find in a school?
    What could you find in your school bag
    What could you find in a zoo?
    What could you find in a park?

(ii) Listening out for a specific word

Read pupil the first line, ask pupil the question.

    Jennifer ate a sandwich.

        'Can you tell me which food word you heard?'

    I ate my breakfast at 8 o'clock

        'Can you tell me which time word you heard?'

    The cat meowed when it was scared

        'Can you tell me which animal word you heard?'

    My sister wore a blue dress

        'Can you tell me what colour word you heard?'

    My birthday is in March

        'Can you tell me which word for a month you heard?'

    The flowers were blue and pink

        'Can you tell me the colour words you heard?'

Copyright material from Catherine Routley (2019), *Special Learners in School*, Routledge

SECTION 1: AUDITORY MEMORY

I felt very sad the other day

'Can you tell me which word you heard telling you about feelings?'

The car went slowly

'Can you tell me which word told you how the car went?'

John was going to the park

'Can you tell me which word told you where John was going?'

Beth and Jane were going to eat hamburger and chips

'Can you tell me the food words you heard?'

(iii) Recap on prepositions using two different ones, using six objects.

'Can you put the … **under** the … and the …. **behind** the ….'

'Can you put the … **under** the … the …. **in front of** the ….'

'Can you put the …. **behind** the …. and the …. **beside** the …. and …'

'Can you put the …. **in front of the** …. and the …. **between the …. and** …. the ….'

'Can you put the … **in** the … and the … **behind** the …?'

'Can you put the … **on** the … and the … **between** the … and the ….?'

'Can you put the … **beside** the …. and the … **under** the …?'

Section 2:
Visual memory

SECTION 2: VISUAL MEMORY

Visual programme Level 2

Activity 1
Placing and finding objects

(i) Adult places four items on the table. Pupil looks at it for ten seconds. Adult removes and asks: 'Can you put the pencils and paper and stapler back in the same place?'

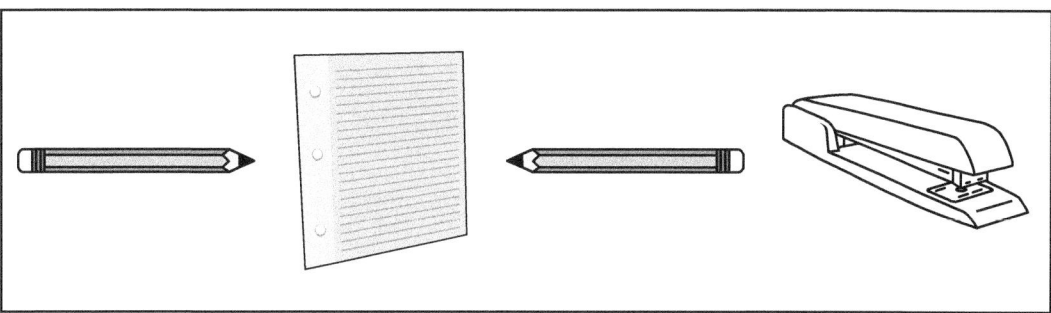

(ii) Adult shows pupil a diagram as shown below for ten seconds, using colours red, blue and yellow for the pattern.

Pupil is presented with a piece of blank squared paper and is asked 'Can you remember where the colours go?' Pupil to use coloured pencils or cubes.

Copyright material from Catherine Routley (2019), *Special Learners in School*, Routledge

(iii) Pupil looks at (a) for ten seconds. Provide pupil with (b) and ask, 'Can you remember where the shapes go on the bag?'

(a) (b)

(iv) Ask pupil to look at the picture below.

Ask pupil, 'In this picture can you find the matching pairs (two which are the same)?'

Copyright material from Catherine Routley (2019), *Special Learners in School*, Routledge

Activity 2
Noting visual details

(i) Adult shows pupil picture below asks: 'Can you look at the picture carefully for ten seconds? I will then ask you questions about it.'

How many boats did you see?

Is there a beach ball in the picture?

Was there someone swimming in the sea?

How many birds are there in the picture?

Did you see a bucket and spade?

Was it a sunny day?

(ii) Show pupil the diagram below for ten seconds and then remove it. Give pupil a sheet of squared paper and ask pupil to reproduce the diagram.

PART 2: LEVEL 2 ACTIVITIES

Activity 3
Visual memory for words and letters

(i) Ask pupil 'Where are the sounds?' Write letter sounds on e.g. stars/circles/triangles and turn them over.

Ask pupil 'Can you find the two sounds that are the same?'

(ii) Visual memory for remembering 'funny' phrases. Pupil is asked to look at a picture and point out the accompanying words.

Only men with black hair can jump over ten lorries

'Can you remember this "funny" sentence?' Pupil engages in another task. Adult asks for repetition after approximately ten minutes. 'Can you remember the "funny" sentence?'

Girls who play football can score eight goals before lunch

Copyright material from Catherine Routley (2019), *Special Learners in School*, Routledge

Pupil engages in another task. Adult asks for repetition after approximately 15 minutes 'Can you remember the "funny" sentence?'

This technique can be useful for remembering facts

Mammals feed their babies on milk

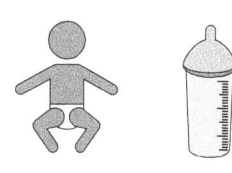

= Mammals

(iii) Picture comparison

(1)   (2)

Pupil is shown both pictures for approximately 15 seconds. Adult then turns pictures so they are faced down. Pupil asked specific questions e.g. 'Is the weather the same in both pictures? Are the shell and crab together in both pictures? Is there a man in both pictures? Are the men in the pictures doing the same thing?'

Activity 4
Recognising identical images

Adult shows card (a) to pupil then places face down. Cards (b) are shown. Ask, 'Can you show me the same picture as this one?', pointing to card (a) which remains face down.

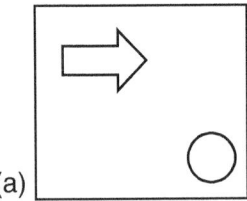

(a)

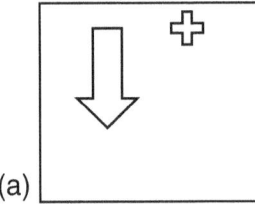

(a)

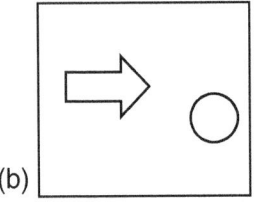 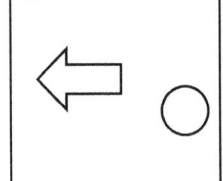

(b)

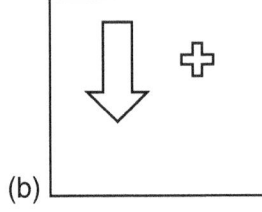 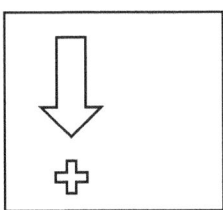

(b)

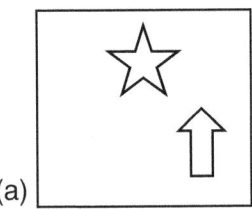

(a)

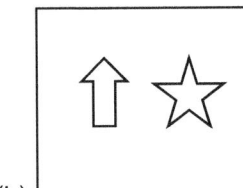 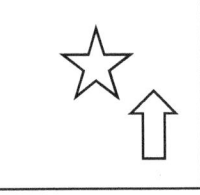

(b)

Copyright material from Catherine Routley (2019), *Special Learners in School*, Routledge

SECTION 2: VISUAL MEMORY

Activity 5
Reproducing images

Adult shows two cards to pupil, removes them and asks, 'Can you draw the pictures on these cards?' (show pupil two blank cards).

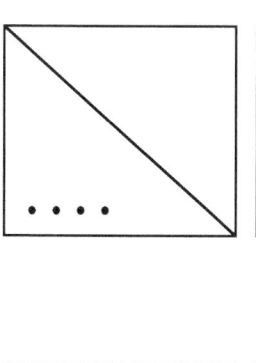 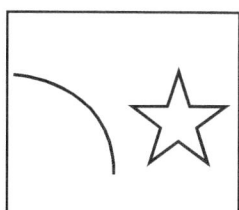 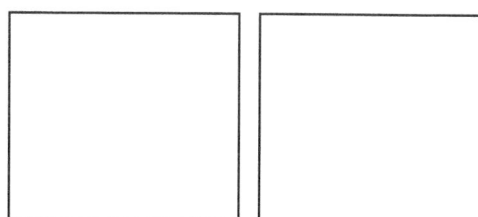

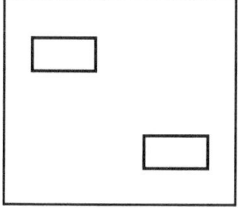 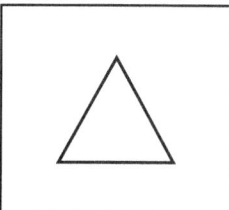 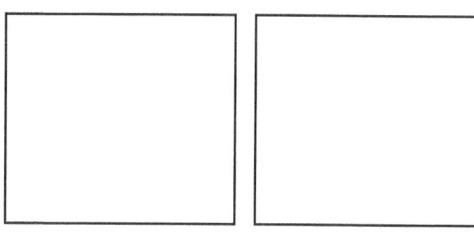

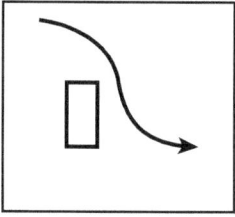 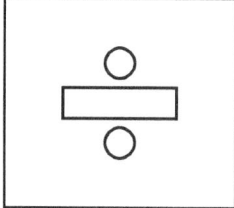 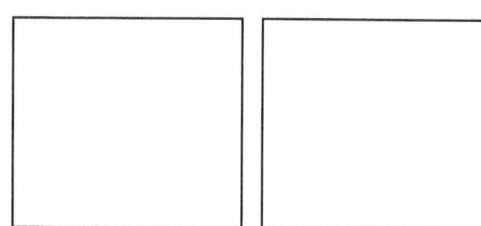

Copyright material from Catherine Routley (2019), *Special Learners in School*, Routledge

Activity 6
Missing numbers and letters

Write in the missing numbers. Pupil is shown card from (a) for five seconds. Provide them with card from (b) and ask, 'Can you put in the missing number or letter?'

(a)

M   S
O

P
C   X

m
s   p

the
e

| 5 6 9 |

8   3
5

(b)

S
O

C   X

s   p

the

| 6 9 |

3
5

Section 3:
Pragmatics

Pragmatics programme Level 2

Activity 1
Logical ordering

(i) Sequencing: The first section on pragmatics focused on the everyday situations faced in the classroom or at home and using the correct language/ behaviours. This section not only relates to the classroom but also includes logical ordering of events, responding to situations, cause and effect, and predicting outcomes.

Ask pupil

You are going to make some toast. What do you do first (choice of two)?

(a) Put the bread in the toaster or   (b) Take the bread from the packet

You are going to draw a picture. What do you need to do this? (Pupil to supply necessary vocabulary e.g. paper, pencil.)

What do you do first?

(a) Begin to draw   (b) Get some paper

You want to eat a bar of chocolate What do you do first?

(a) Put it in your mouth   (b) Pull the wrapper off the bar

When you get to the swimming pool. What do you do first?

(a) Jump into the water   (b) Get changed

You want a turn on the slide. What do you do first?

(a) Go down the slide   (b) Go up the slide

Copyright material from Catherine Routley (2019), *Special Learners in School*, Routledge

(ii) Ask pupil 'What do you think could have happened before … (choice of two)?'

John was watching television and he started to laugh

   (a) He saw something funny   (b) He ate a biscuit

A cat ran up the tree. What do you think could have happened before?

   (a) A dog chased him, and he was frightened   (b) He drank some milk

Paul was late for school. What do you think could have happened before?

   (a) The bus got stuck in traffic   (b) He hadn't finished his homework last night

(iii) Ask pupil 'What could have happened before... (no choice)?'

James felt so full up, he had to sit down.

Karen was completely out of breath and panting.

After the match everyone was congratulating Matthew on beating the school record.

Activity 2
Predicting events

(i) Ask pupil

'Would you get into trouble if …. (choice of three)?'

You ran in the hall when you were told to walk quietly.
You made your friends laugh in class.
You were very helpful to the teacher.

'Would you get into trouble if …?'

You helped your friend when he fell over in the playground.
You copied your test from your friend.
You threw coats on the floor.

'What would do you think would happen if … (without choice)?'

You didn't bring a coat and it started to rain

You forgot your homework

You didn't want to get out of bed to go to school

You cut your finger when cutting through an apple

(ii) Ask pupil

'Can you tell me which one you like best and why?'

A cricket ball or a football

A bicycle or a scooter

A dog or a cat

Milk or juice

Popcorn or crisps

Copyright material from Catherine Routley (2019), *Special Learners in School*, Routledge

(iii) Sentence completion

Adult to pupil: 'I am going to start a sentence. Can you finish it with one or two words so that it makes sense?'

I would like to see …

I like the colour …

On Sunday I like to …

For breakfast I eat …

I am fed up when …

At school I really enjoy …

My favourite drink is …

I feel scared when …

My favourite animal is …

Activity 3
Predicting reactions and feelings

(i) Read sentences to pupil and then ask pupil **'What's going to happen?'**

John's team is playing in the final of the football tournament, but he feels ill. Do you think he will play?

Katie and her friends were talking excitedly in the library. The librarian is getting annoyed. Do you think she will tell them off? What do you think she will say?

Jake has lost his maths book for the second time. Will his teacher be cross? What do you think she will say to him?

Zac is being silly at lunch time and is eating others' food from their plates to annoy them. The supervisor has seen him and is coming over. Do you think she will be very cross? What do you think she will say?

(ii) Read sentences to pupil and ask pupil **'How do others feel?'**

Your brother got an A in his maths test. How does he feel?
What would you say to him?

Your friend tried out for the netball/soccer team and didn't get chosen. How do they feel?
What could you say to him/her to make them feel a little better?

Jennifer's cat died over the weekend and she told you about it.
How do you think she feels?
What could you say to her?

Jonathan is playing by himself in the playground.
How do you think he feels ….?
What could you say to him to make him feel better?

Jen's mum told her they won't be going on holiday this year. How do you think she feels?
What could you say to her to help her feel a little better?

Copyright material from Catherine Routley (2019), *Special Learners in School*, Routledge

Activity 4
Asking simple questions

Adult to pupil: 'I am going to say some sentences. Can you listen carefully and finish the sentence with one word? Listen for the important word in the sentence'

(i) I like to watch *Superman*.   Do you like to watch *Superman*?

I like short hair.   Do you like short (hair)?

I don't like swimming.   Do you like (swimming)?

John can run fast.   Can you run very (fast)?

In the cinema I eat popcorn.   Do you eat (popcorn) in the cinema?

(ii) Adult to pupil: 'This time I am going to say two words and ask you finish the sentence.'

I like pizza and chips.   Do you like (pizza and chips)?

I want to be good at football and tennis.   Do you want to be good at (football and tennis)?

I like to drink milkshakes and juice.   Do you like to drink (milkshakes and juice)?

When it snows I love to play snowball fights.   Do you like to play (snowball fights)?

(iii) Responding to a situation: 'Can you tell me why you think this has happened?'

Your pencil breaks when you start to write (choice of two)

    They're not made properly   You hold it too tight and push too hard

You want to paint a picture with lots of colours in it but the colours become messy and go into each other. Why do you think this happened?

    You haven't waited for them to dry   The paintbrush is too wet

The children in Class 2 planted some beans but they were all dried up the following week. Why?

    The insects ate them   They forgot to water them

You spilled some your orange juice on the table. What would you do?

    Ask for a cloth to wipe it up   Put your finger in it

Copyright material from Catherine Routley (2019), *Special Learners in School*, Routledge

Activity 5
(a) What's the right word?
(b) What's the right question to ask?

(a) **What's the right word?**

Ask pupil **'Can you tell me the right word to finish these sentences so that they make sense?'**

(If pupil finds it difficult to think of an appropriate word, provide the choice from two for each sentence)

I like milk on my cereal. I eat my cereal with a ……..

Spoon   or   fork

I want to read a book. I will borrow one from the ….

Supermarket   or   library

It is Jennifer's birthday tomorrow. I must bake her a …

Cake   or   dress

I am going to paint a picture of my holidays. I will need my …

Pencils   or   paints

Yesterday I had a toothache and had to visit

The dentist   or   the hairdressers

Oh, dear it's raining I will need to take my

Sun hat   or   umbrella

Copyright material from Catherine Routley (2019), *Special Learners in School*, Routledge

(b) What's the right question to ask?

Ask pupil **'Can you tell me the question you would ask to get the following answers?'**

I just got a new kitten for my birthday

My birthday is next week

I went to the cinema and watched my favourite film last Sunday

I am going to see my favourite team play football tomorrow

I feel so tired today

I had an awful meal last night

I had sausage and chips last night

Yes, I'm going to Maggie's party

I'm going to McDonald's after school

I'm wearing my new jumper tomorrow

I will be 8 next month

I don't think I'm going to football practice

Activity 6
Starting a conversation

(i) Ask pupil 'Can you tell me what would you say if I said …?'

Hello …..

How are things going ……?

What's your name ……?

What's going on ….?

When are you coming back?

How are you?

I must go now

See you next Monday

What's the date today?

I like your drawing ….

You're a very fast runner

(ii) Inference without choice

Ask pupil 'I am going to tell you about problems that happened. Can you tell me what you think made them happen in the first place?'

I came into my house soaking wet. What do you think could have happened?

Mum opened her shopping bag and there was a lot of juice at the bottom of her bag. What could have happened?

The school fire alarm went. What could have happened?

John was sent outside the classroom. What could have happened?

Chris felt sick after the picnic. What could have happened?

Mike was sunburned after a day on the beach. What could have happened?

Jacob came into class after break time with a cut knee. What could have happened?

After saying yes, Pete's mother said he couldn't have a sleepover with his friends. What could have happened?

I looked for my lunch box but it wasn't there. What could have happened?

My toast got burned. What could have happened.?

Kieran looked for his bicycle after school, but it was missing. What could have happened?

You ate two packets of crisps and a bar of chocolate and then you went on the roundabout. You were sick afterwards. Why do you think this happened?

I went to buy some milk and couldn't find my money. What could have happened?

Dad was in a panic as he couldn't find his car keys. What could have happened?

Part 3
Additional ideas for working with pupils

The following section does not form part of the programme as such. It provides guidelines on several important areas – reading, differentiation, picture description and inferencing. There will be pupils for whom the ideas will be too difficult/easy, but they should be seen as a starting point for practitioners to extend and adapt.

Reading a new book

The busy classroom often entails children moving on to a reading book without there being time to provide essential first introduction to the book. Admittedly working through that first introduction with a pupil can be a little time consuming, but it provides the pupil with the confidence and background knowledge to a simple story, providing important top-down information to facilitate the reading process. It also provides practice in prediction, sequencing and introduces reasoning skills. I have used an example here from the *Oxford reading tree Level 4 red*. Shown below is a suggestion of exchanges between adult and pupil. Responses from pupils will obviously vary.

Adult: 'This book is called "Stuck in the Mud". Can you see why it is called that?'
(Possible response: child points to picture of sheep stuck in the mud)

Adult 'If you're stuck in something can you get out?'
(Possible response: 'No'/shakes head)

'Look at the picture of the family. Do they look worried the sheep is stuck?
(Possible response: 'Yes'/nods)

'We have met these children and their dog before. Can you remember their names?'
(Pupil is probably familiar with these from previous books in the series but may need prompting)

Look through the book with the pupil, talking about the pictures and providing opportunities for prediction.

'What do you think Chip can hear? Let's see if you're right.'

'Do you think they can pull the sheep out of the mud?'

'Look at dad's face. How do you think dad feels going in to the mud, do you think he likes it?'
(Always provide pupil with relevant vocabulary.)

Give book to pupil, suggested questions:

'Can you find me the first picture showing the sheep stuck in the mud?'

'Can you find the picture where the sheep is being pulled out of the mud?'

'Can you tell me what happened in the last picture?'

'By looking at the pictures can you tell me what happens in the story?'

(The pupil is thoroughly familiar with the story and, using a knowledge of the content matter and vocabulary, together with early phonic skills, the reading experience should be easier.)

Differentiation and comprehension

The different levels of abilities within the mainstream classroom have meant that differentiation is increasing in importance. The goal of teachers is to make the curriculum accessible to all students.

When considering differentiating, three concepts have to be kept in mind:

- What is the main point of the piece of text?
- Which are the peripheral points which are superfluous to the main points and are not essential to understanding of the text?
- How can the main points be understood and recorded?

Some general points which should be considered when differentiating:

- Enlarge the font of the text
- Use double spacing
- Insert images.

The following example illustrates two suggestions for modifying a history lesson for KS2 Year 3

(a) Original text   (b) modified   (c) modified for pupils with more significant learning difficulties.

Comprehension exercise

Roman entertainment

(a) Original text

Although people in Roman times did not have much spare time as they were too busy working one of the activities they really enjoyed was watching men and animals fighting. These fights were between wild animals, gladiators and wild animals and gladiator against gladiator. Rich and poor would pile into the amphitheatre to witness these bloodthirsty scenes.

They went to an amphitheatre called the Coliseum. This was a large outdoor theatre where all sorts of animals (such as wild cats, buffaloes, bears, elephants and lions) were kept in cages below and then made to fight one another. The Romans were very inventive, and they came up with lots of different ways in which the crowd could get their fix of combat and bloodshed. A Roman gladiator was an ancient professional fighter who fought with weapons and armour. Without doubt, gladiator spectacles were one of the most watched forms of popular entertainment in the Roman world. Famous gladiators had a huge following and it could be said their life was a dangerous but exciting one. Many gladiators were the Roman equivalent of 'cannon fodder' – there to entertain and be killed and in fact they were slaves, former slaves or condemned prisoners. As the fights were usually to the death, the gladiators had a short life expectancy. When a gladiator was beaten (but had not died) the audience would wave their scarves or give the thumbs up sign if they wanted him to live or thumbs down if they wanted him killed. The casualty rate per 'show' was massive – nearly fifty per cent died during each show Not all gladiators used the same weapons, for example a gladiator with a sword and shield might fight another with a spear called a trident and a net.

Copyright material from Catherine Routley (2019), *Special Learners in School*, Routledge

PART 3: ADDITIONAL IDEAS FOR WORKING WITH PUPILS

Questions

What do you understand by the term 'cannon fodder'?

Do you think 'entertainment' is the right word to use for the fights in the Coliseum?

What do you think 'get their fix of combat and bloodshed' means?

What is another word for 'combat'?

Can you find out what a trident looks like and draw a picture of one.

Do you think the life of a gladiator was exciting ?

(b) Differentiated comprehension

People in Roman times did not have much spare time as they were too busy working, but something they really enjoyed was watching fights between gladiators

and fights between people and animals. Rich and poor would rush to a large outdoor theatre, amphitheatre called the Coliseum.

Copyright material from Catherine Routley (2019), *Special Learners in School*, Routledge

Many different animals were used to fight each other, wild cats, buffaloes, bears, elephants, lions.

It was not only animals who fought each other. Many people who came to the Coliseum came to see fights between the gladiators. When a gladiator was beaten (but had not died) the audience would wave their scarves or give the thumbs up sign if they wanted him to live, or thumbs down for him to be killed.

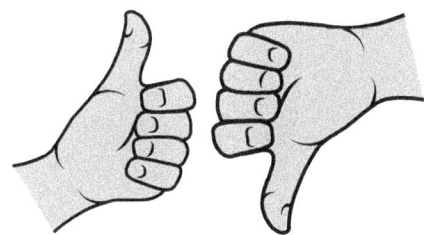

The gladiators were often slaves or prisoners from the many wars fought by the Romans and sometimes almost half of them died during these fights with each other. Many of the gladiators became famous but while their life may have been exciting, it was very dangerous.

Further questions

Was the Coliseum an indoor or outdoor theatre?

Can you write three types of wild animals who fought each other?

Can you draw a picture of the sign the Romans used meaning the Gladiator could live?

Do you think the gladiator had a very dangerous life?

Is this right? The Romans came to the Coliseum only to see wild animals fight.

(c) Differentiation for a pupil with significant learning needs

Show pupils the pictures.

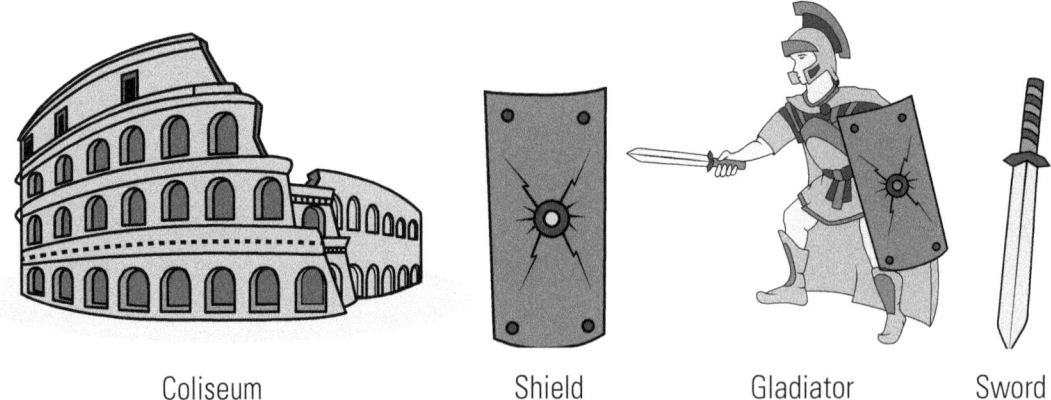

Coliseum　　　　　Shield　　　　　Gladiator　　　　　Sword

In Roman times people went to a large outdoor theatre called the Coliseum. They watched wild animals and gladiators fighting. Gladiators were very famous fighters, but their lives were very dangerous. Almost half of them were killed every time there was a show.

Questions

A Roman who made his living from fighting was called a _____?

The Coliseum was an _____ _____ theatre?

Can you label the gladiator's helmet sword and shield?

Put a circle around the animals you think would have been used in the fighting in the Coliseum.

Copyright material from Catherine Routley (2019), *Special Learners in School*, Routledge

Describing a picture

When a pupil is asked to describe a picture, sometimes the content can be overpowering and there is a tendency to focus on the most visual aspect e.g. park, with the verb often omitted.

It is often necessary to 'break down' the picture by using visuals along with the familiar who? what? where? questions.

Who is this?
A boy

What's he doing?
walking

Where?
in the park

Adding on further details, e.g. a 'what?' question.

Who is this?   What is he doing?   What is this?

A boy   is eating   an ice cream

Where?

On the   beach

Learning to read with symbols

For some pupils with special needs, using symbols together with print which is subsequently removed can act as a prop to word recognition.

Jason   blew   the   candles   out   on   his   cake

The next step would be a sentence with the smaller images and larger text.

Jason blew out the candles on his cake

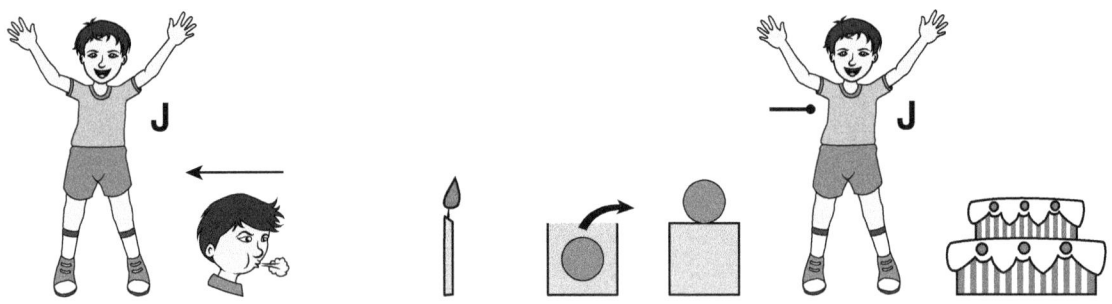

Symbols are finally removed.

Jason blew out the candles on his cake

Inference skills

This is an important skill in helping children to achieve text comprehension; a task which is challenging for pupils and not only those with special needs.

There are various steps to helping a child achieve this, and by focusing in the early stages on the visual, this can give confidence to the pupil.

Using a large picture with a question which relies totally on the visual

Do you think the picture shows children in the summer or winter?

Why do you think that?

Can you tell me what is missing in these pictures?

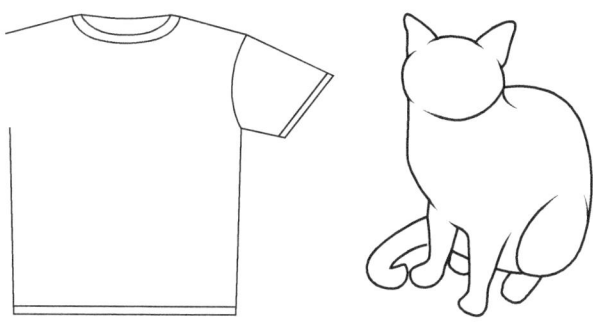

Sequencing:

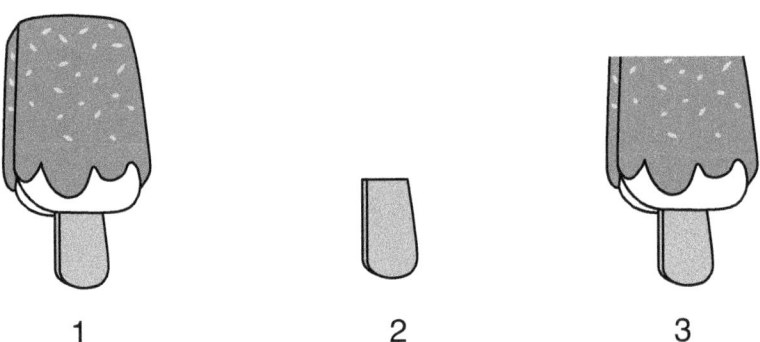

Do you think the pictures are in the right order? Where do you think they should be?

What do you think will happen to the cake now the candles are lit?

What do you think happened in the missing picture? (Prompt if required, 'Where do you think the dog went after eating his food?)

Show pupil one image, ask pupil one question.

Who do you think made these dirty footprints?

Progress to two questions.

Where do you think the boy is going? Why is he running?

When ready, ask pupil three questions.

Do you think it's a maths or English class where the boy is working?

Do you think he is finding the work easy or hard?

How do you know?

Then without picture. Ask pupil, **'What could they be talking about?'**

Mum came in from shopping 'Can you put these in the freezer now or else they will melt'

'Don't eat too many of these, it's not good for your teeth.'

'I think the chocolate flavour is the best'

'I like coke, milk and juice'

'That was a free kick'

'It's very cold outside'

'We need to peel it first'

'Let's pick them and put them in a vase'

Ask pupil, '**Where am I?**'

Jane sat in the chair and waited for the lady to cut her hair

Peter waited for the boy on the swing to finish

'A hamburger with chips please'

Mum is pushing a trolley and we have lots of food in it

We are waiting quietly for the Head teacher to start

I jumped into the water and made a big splash

I am lying in the sun and can smell the sea

The lights have gone down and we are waiting for the film to start.

Learners with significant behaviour/language needs

When working with pupils with behaviour needs, such as an attention deficit, poor eye contact, using gesture or Makaton, encountered in the mainstream, the following ideas may be helpful.

Should the pupil be unable to use symbols as a communication aid it is necessary to use objects of reference alongside the sign to indicate timetable changes e.g. a spoon to indicate lunch time, Lego® to indicate free play, a pencil representing colouring/writing.

Once the pupil has some understanding of the connection, the object should be placed on a piece of card with a picture of what the object of reference represents. An example of communicating lunch time is shown in image (a). Once the connection is secure, the actual object can be dispensed with. The next step is to ensure the sign/symbol on its own is understood. To help achieve this, a card with the representational symbol, together with a picture of the sign itself is used. This is shown in image (b). It is necessary to always use sign in communication. The aim is for the child to communicate by basic sign and where necessary to use symbols contained in a personal communication book.

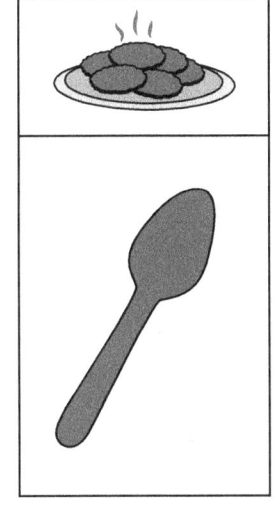
(a)

(b)

The important objective is to gain the pupil's attention and for him/her to look for communication. If a sign is used, it should be basic in the first instance. only the object referred to should be signed e.g. spoon – dinner. Do not use modifiers, for example, colours at this stage. Reciprocity is essential to establish. Turn taking should be confined to 'you' or 'me'.

Rewards are important but it is essential these are not given too readily because an obsession towards the reward can develop.